I0439339

Cute FLOWERS

GRAYSCALE COLORING BOOKS

VOLUME 3.

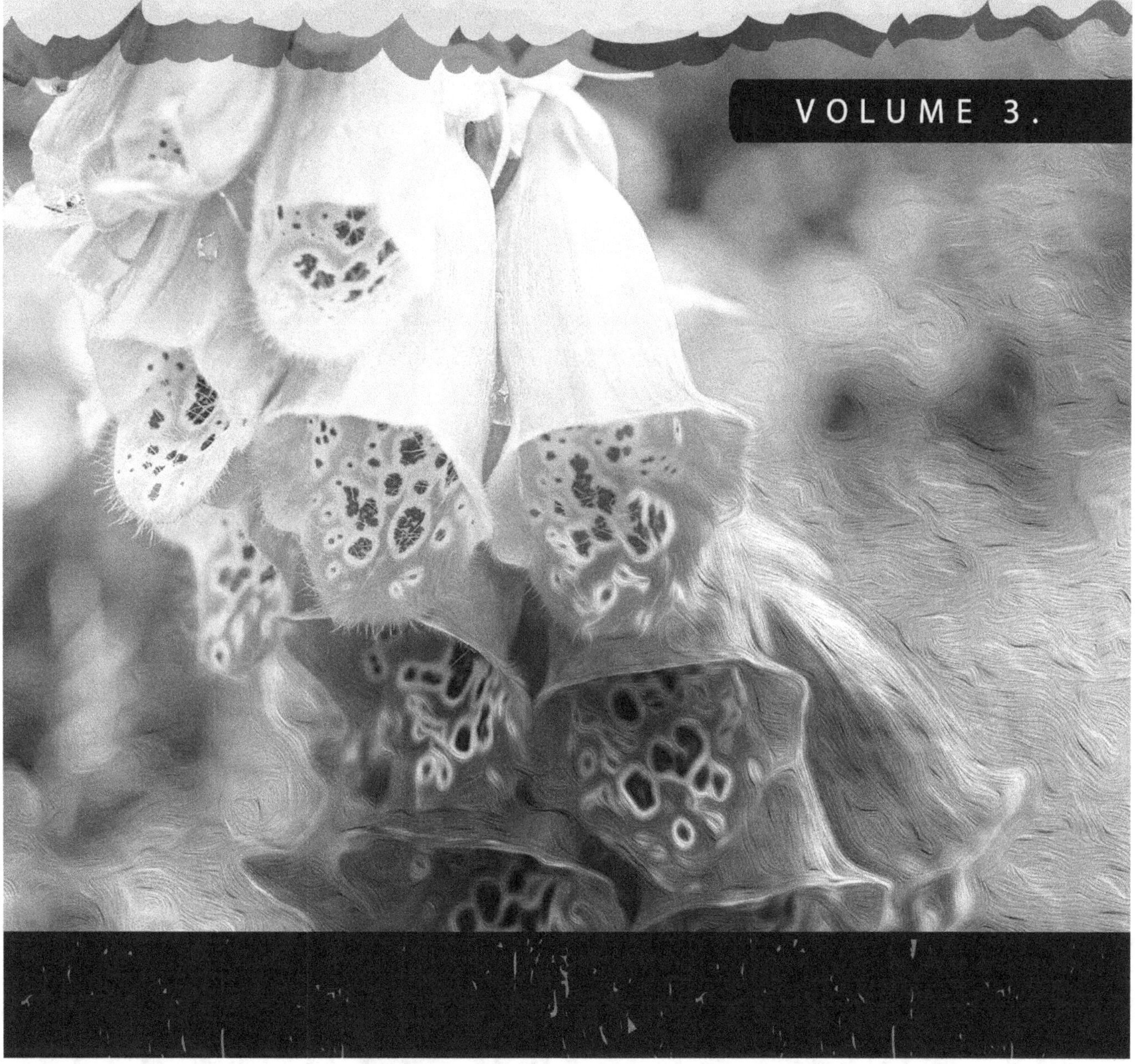

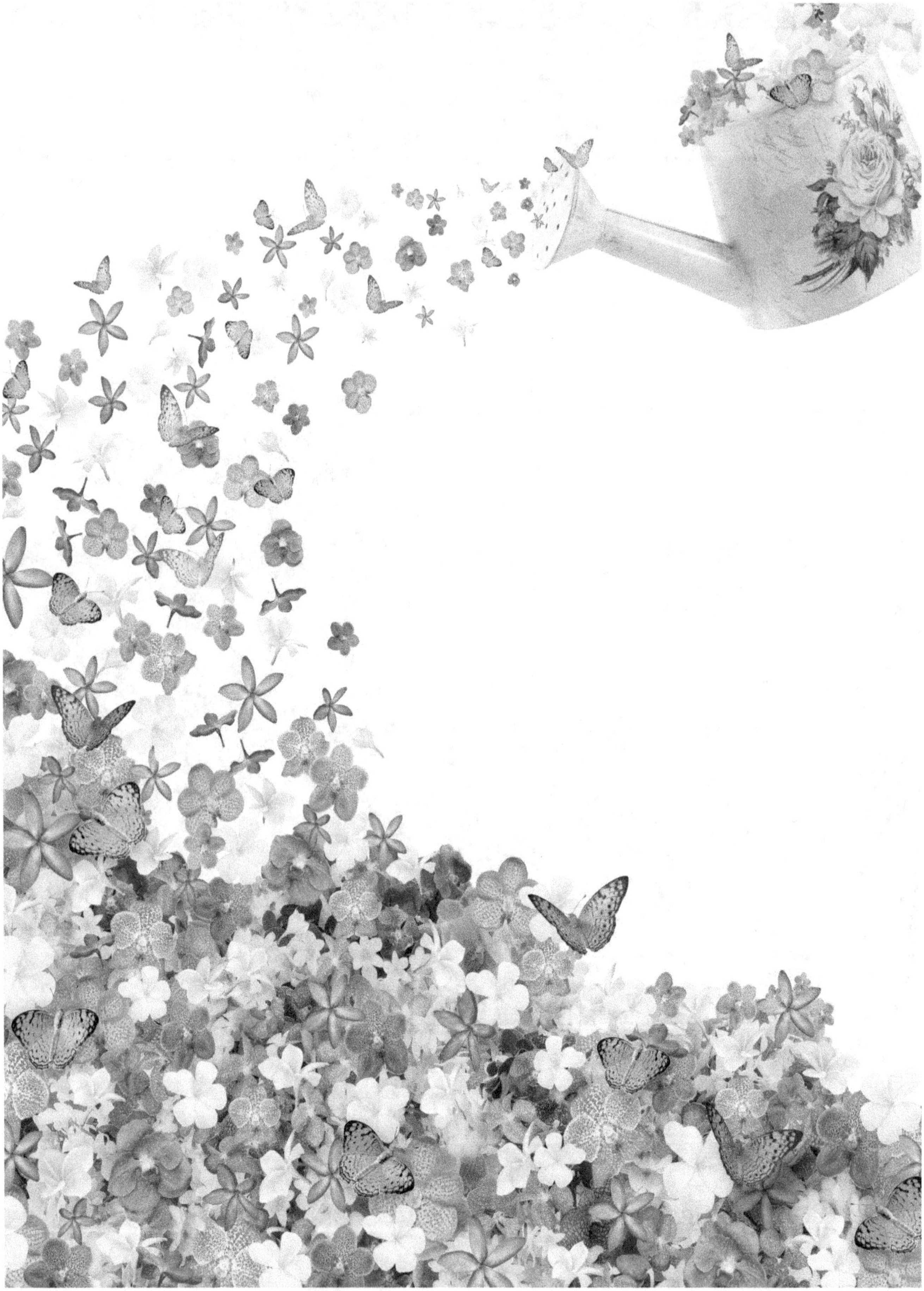

COLOR TEST PAGE

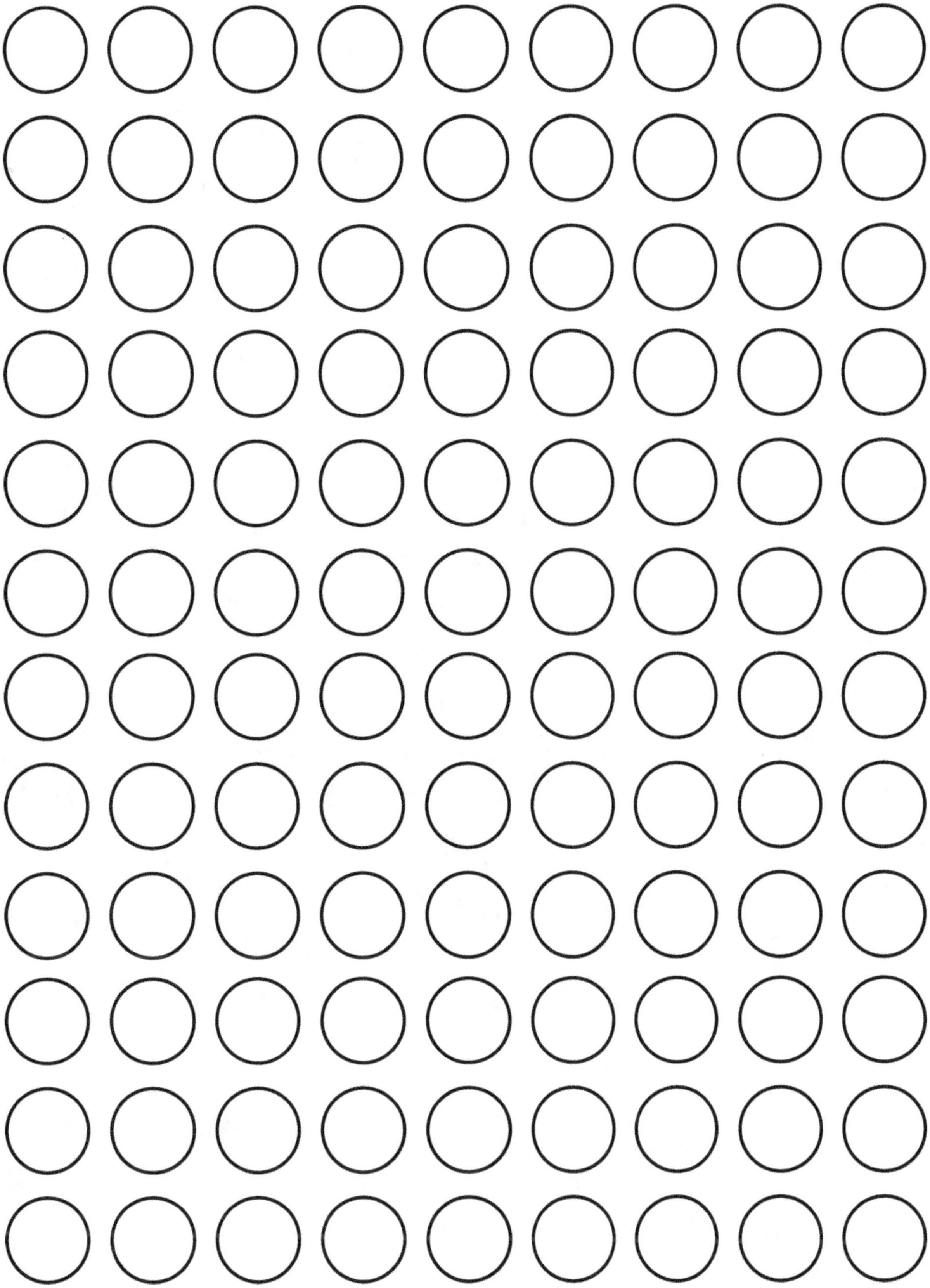

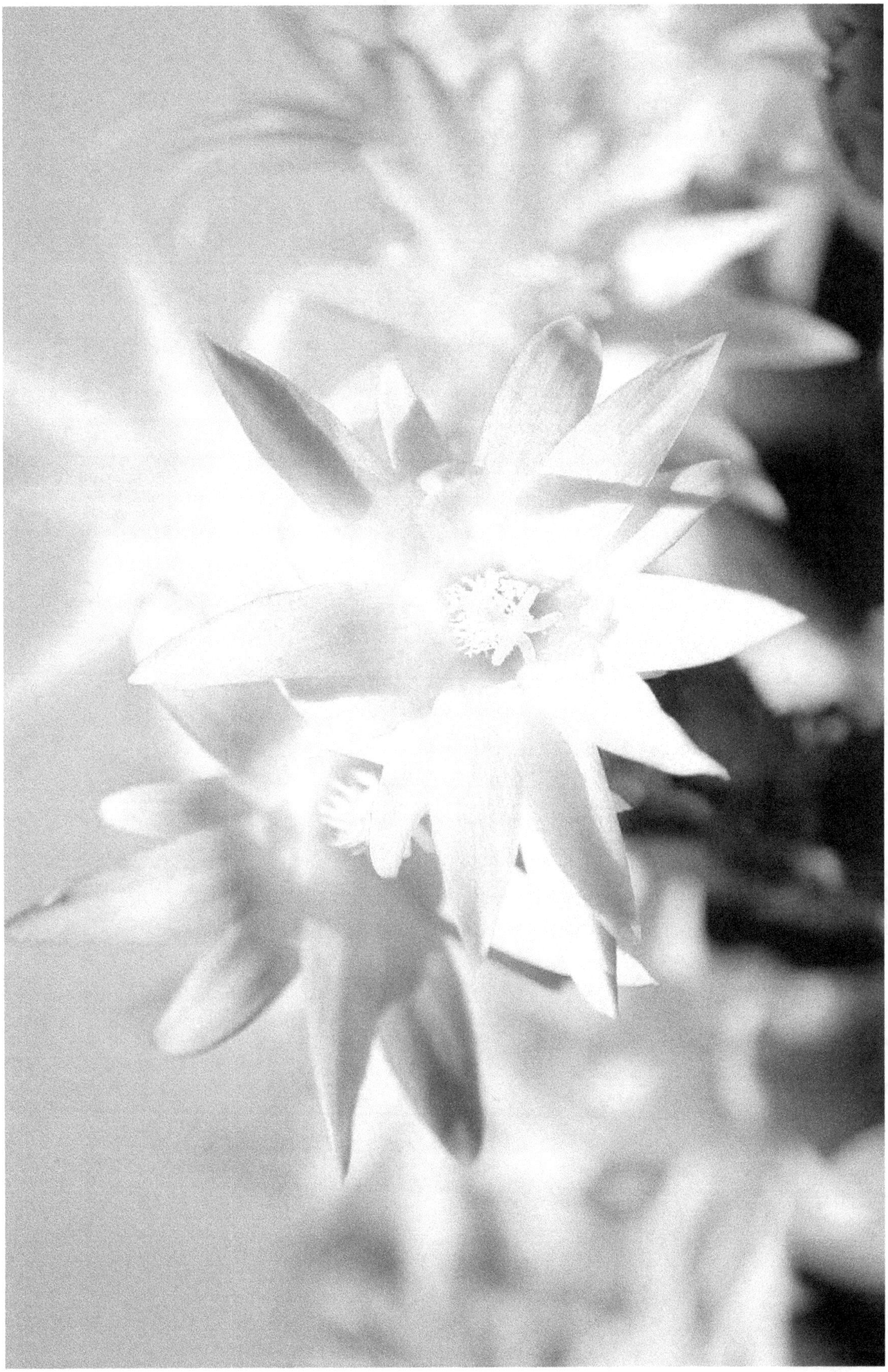

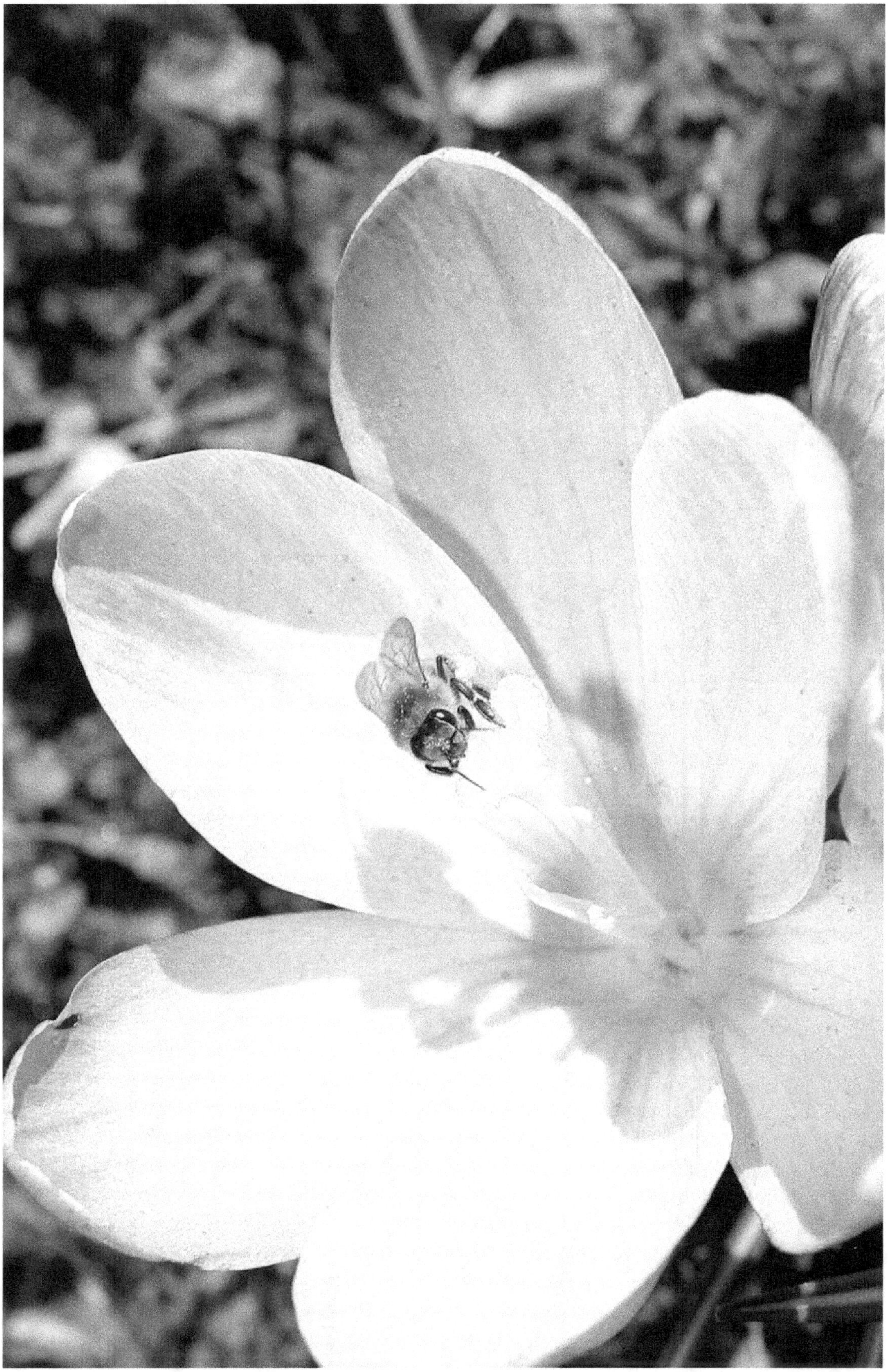

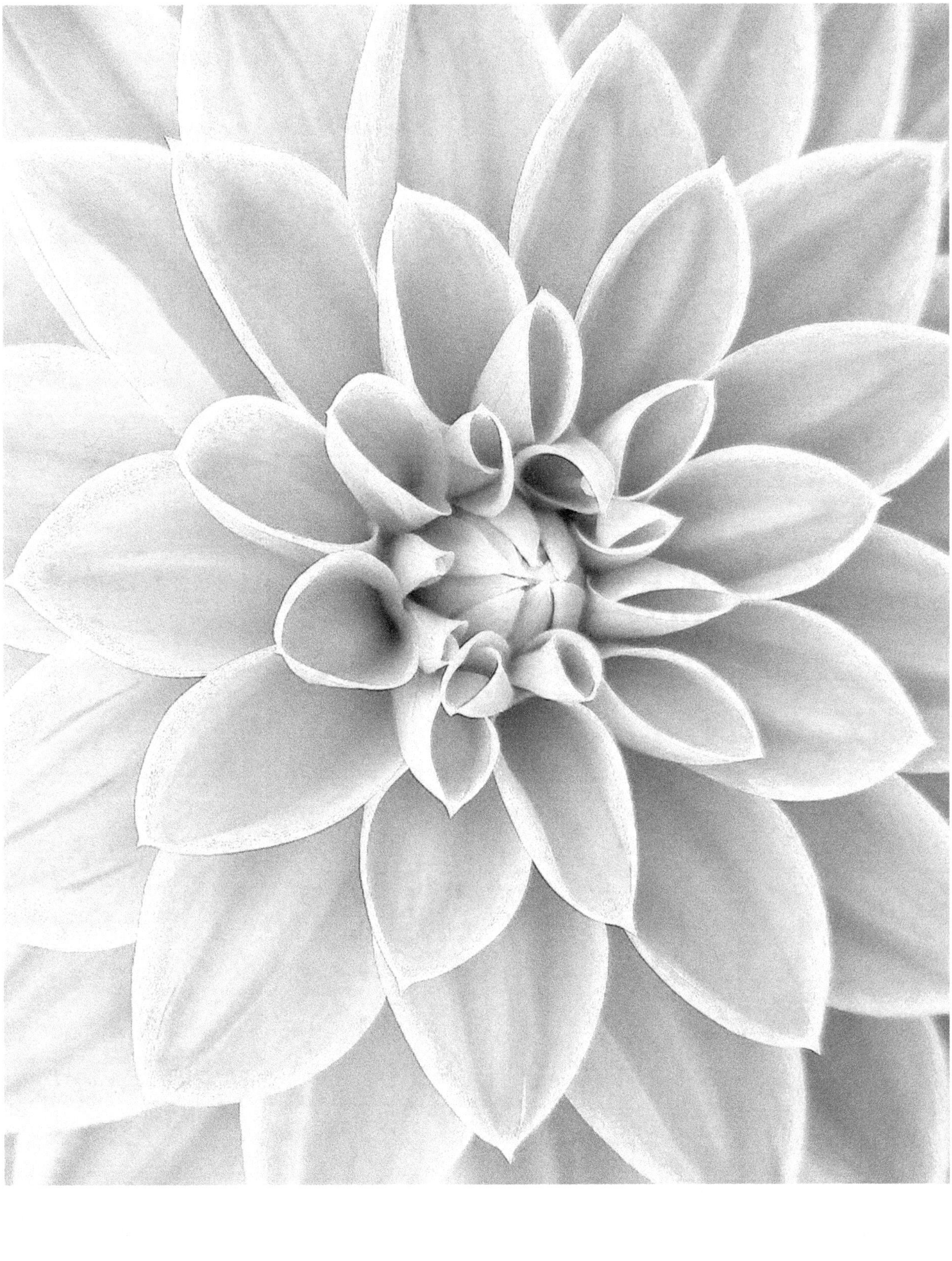

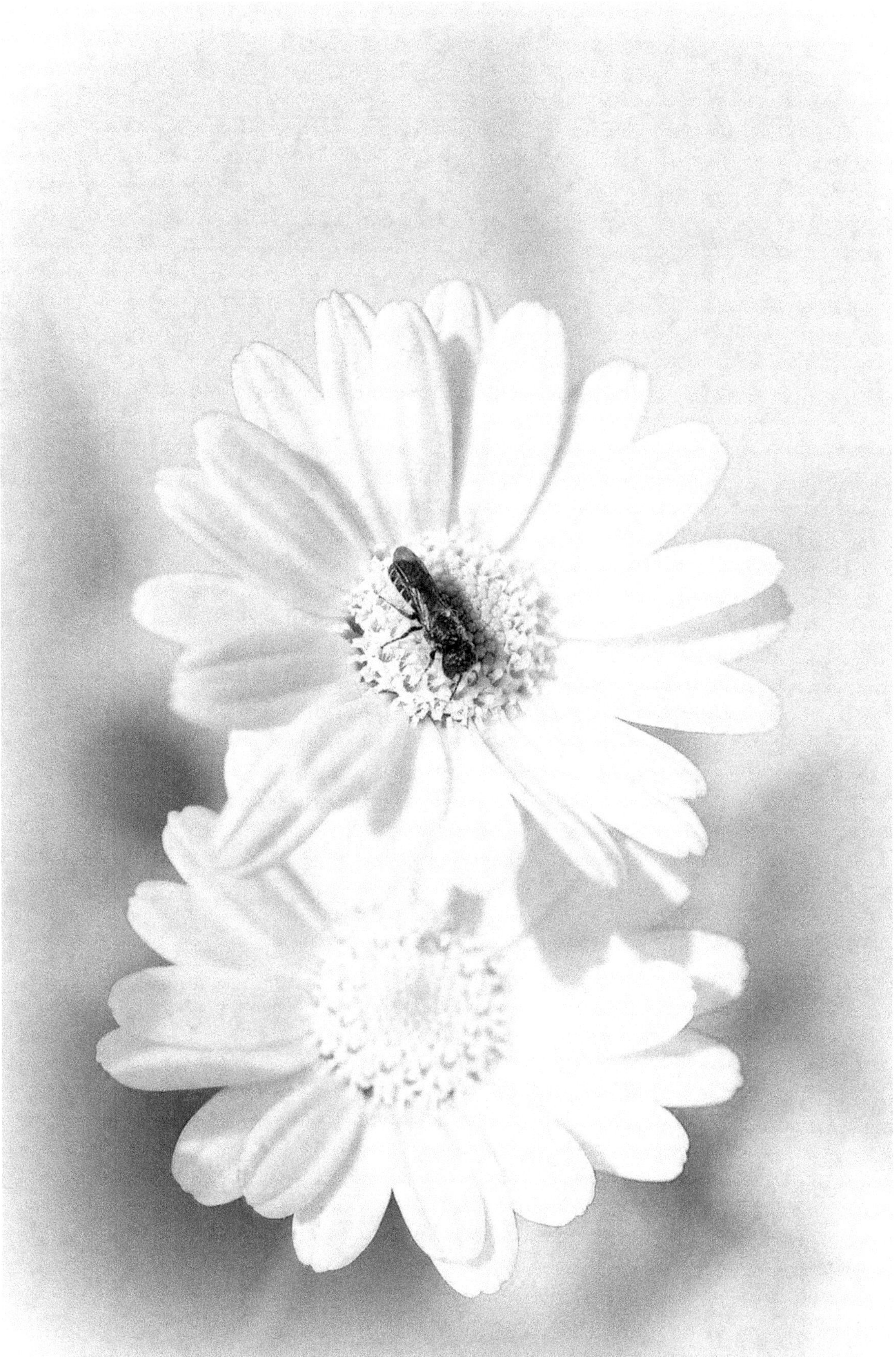

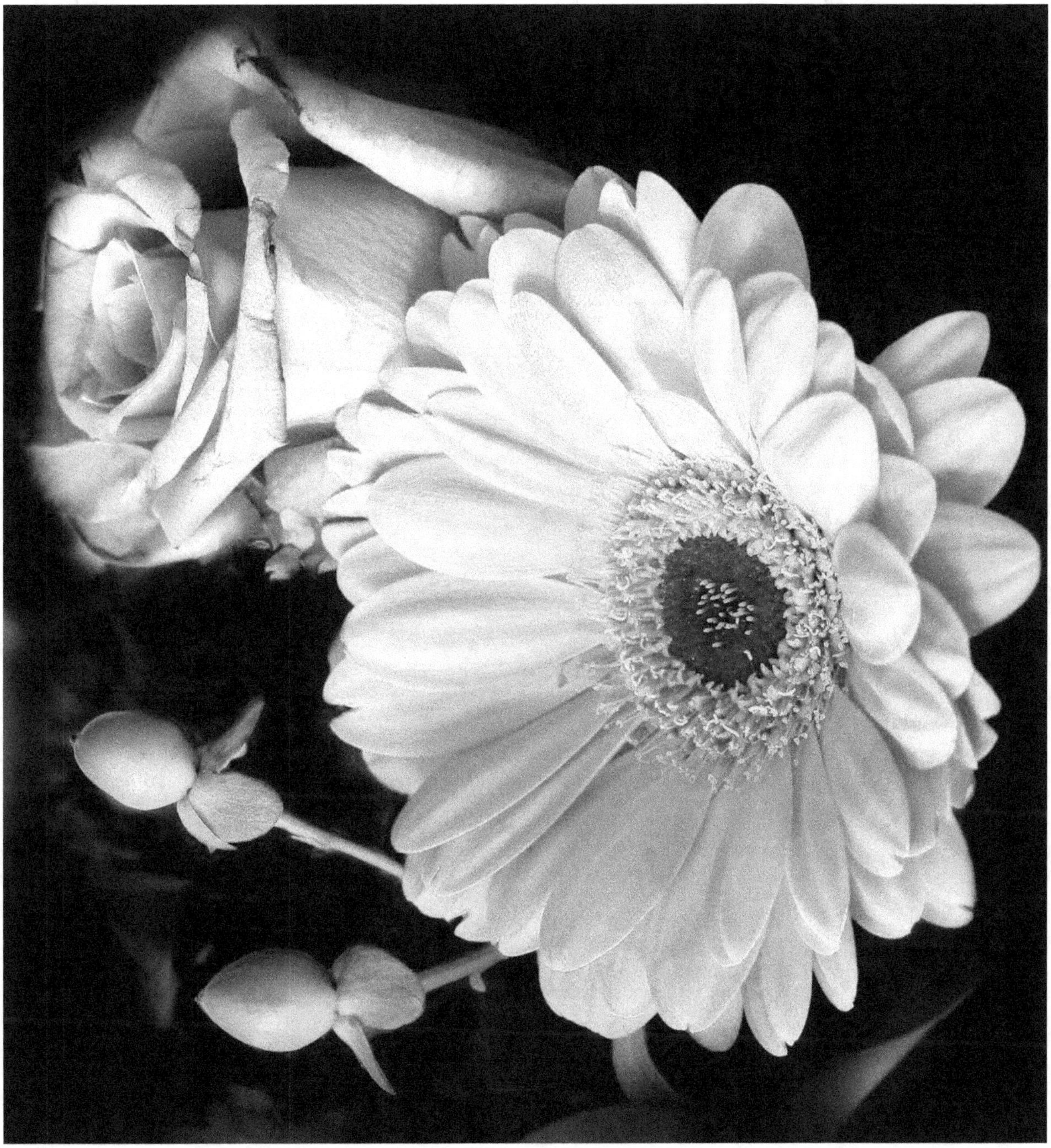

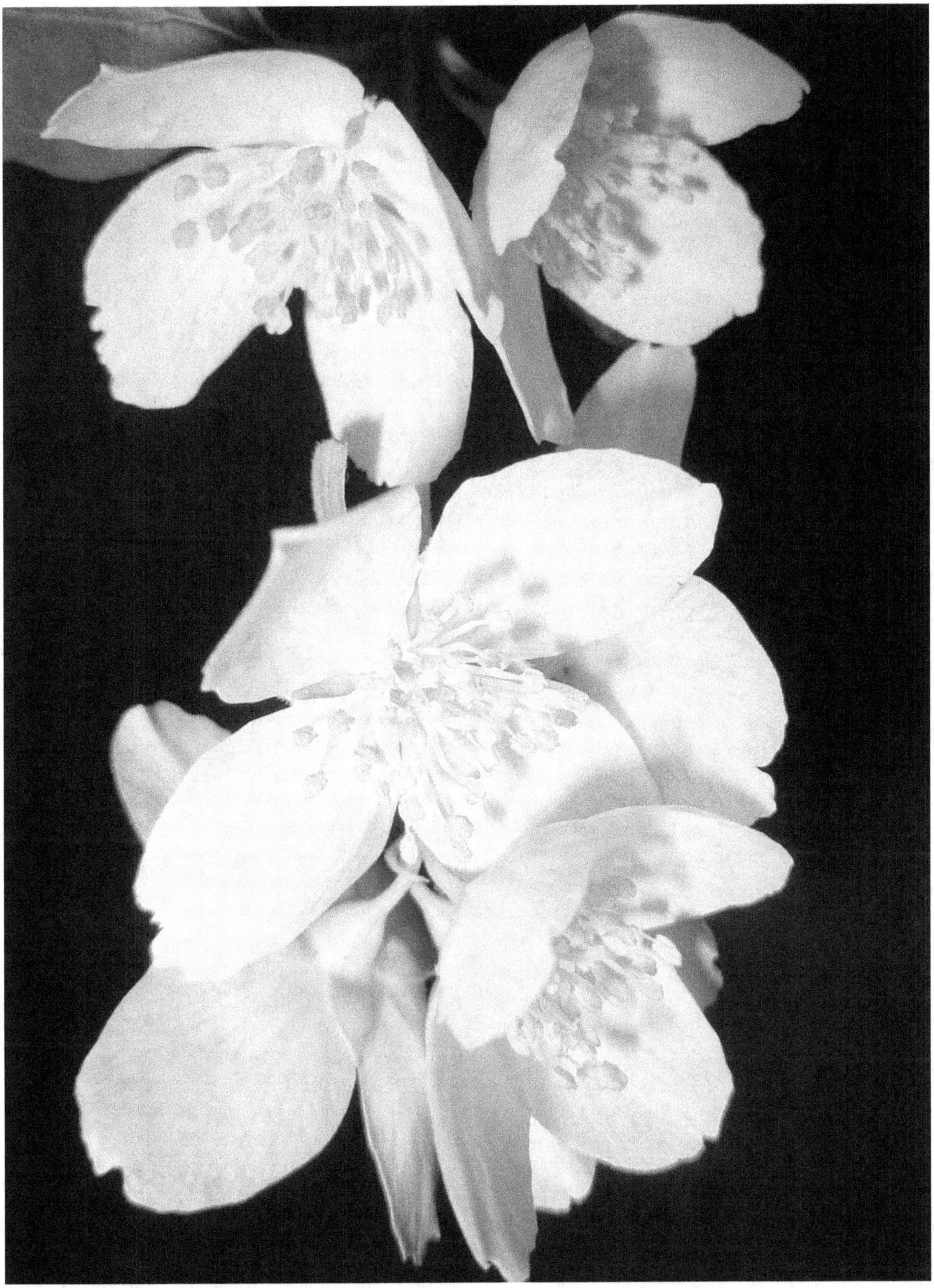

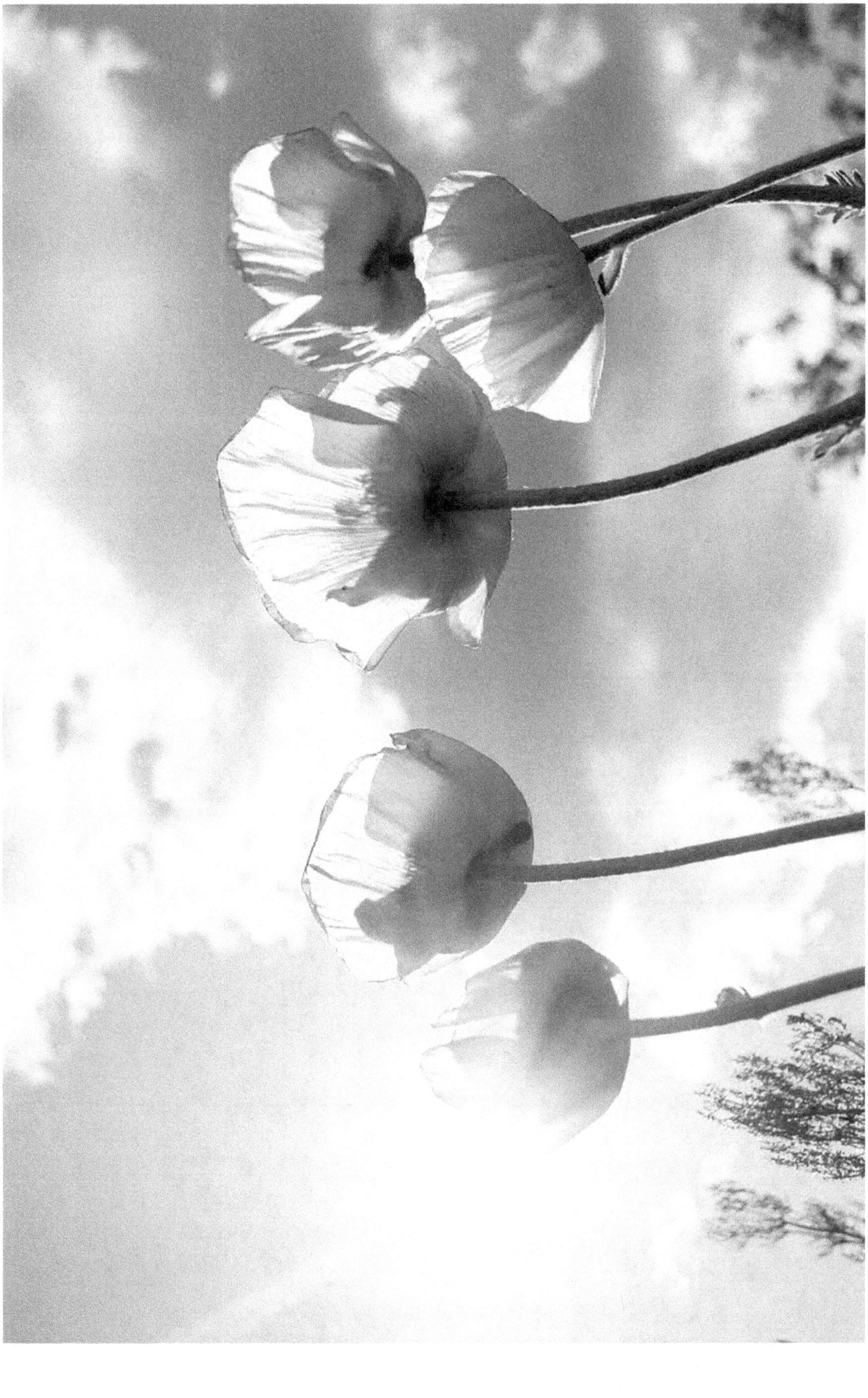

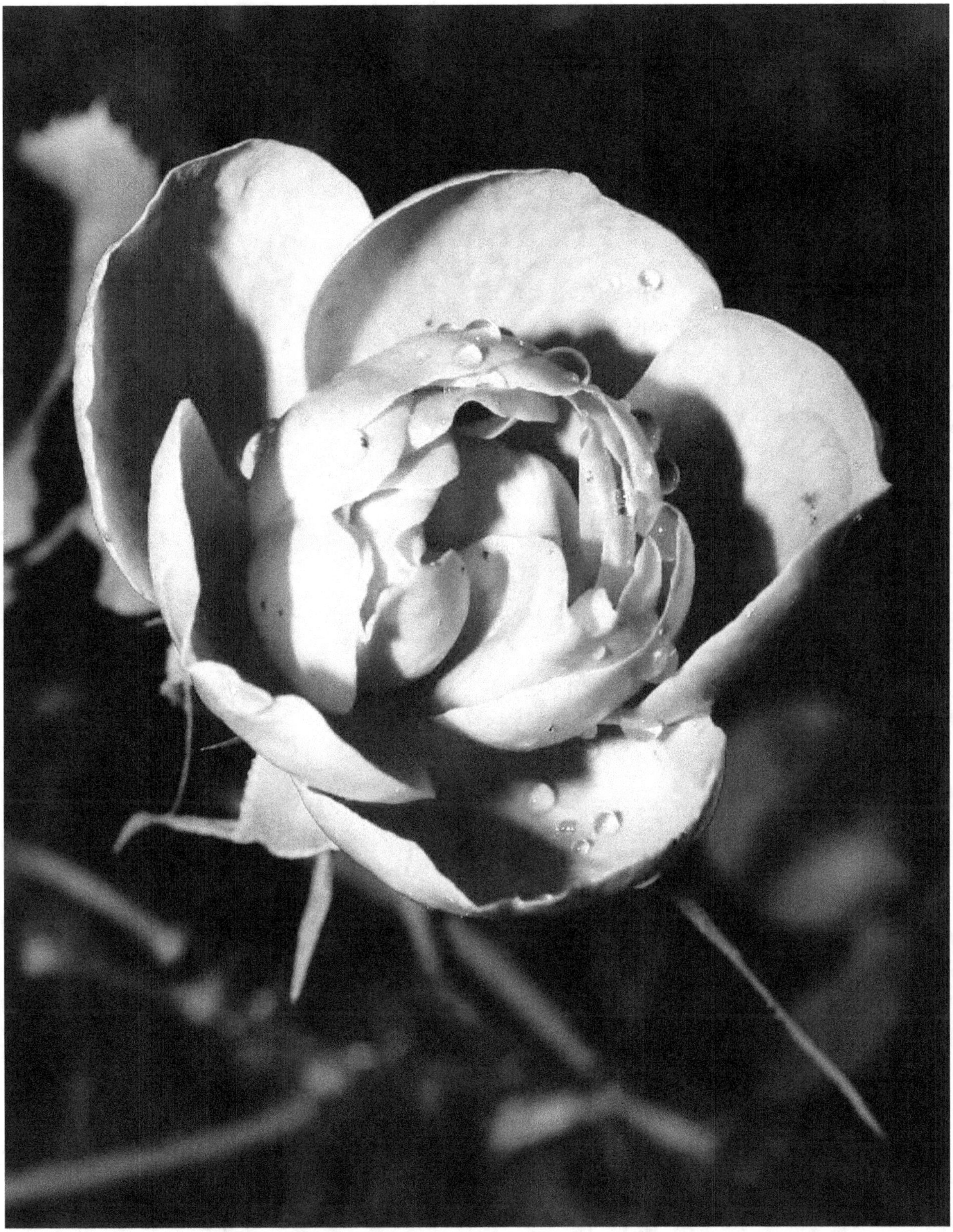

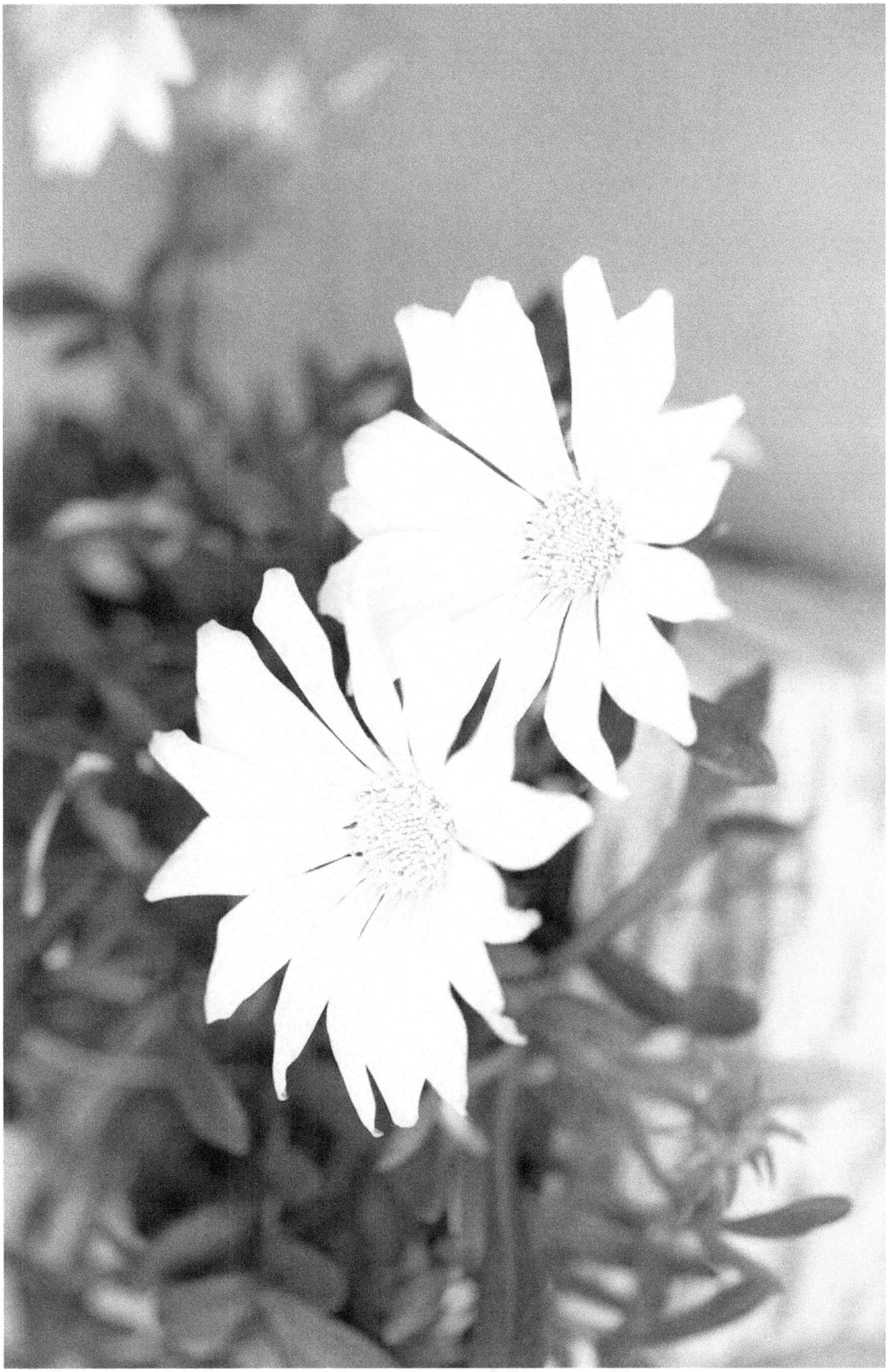

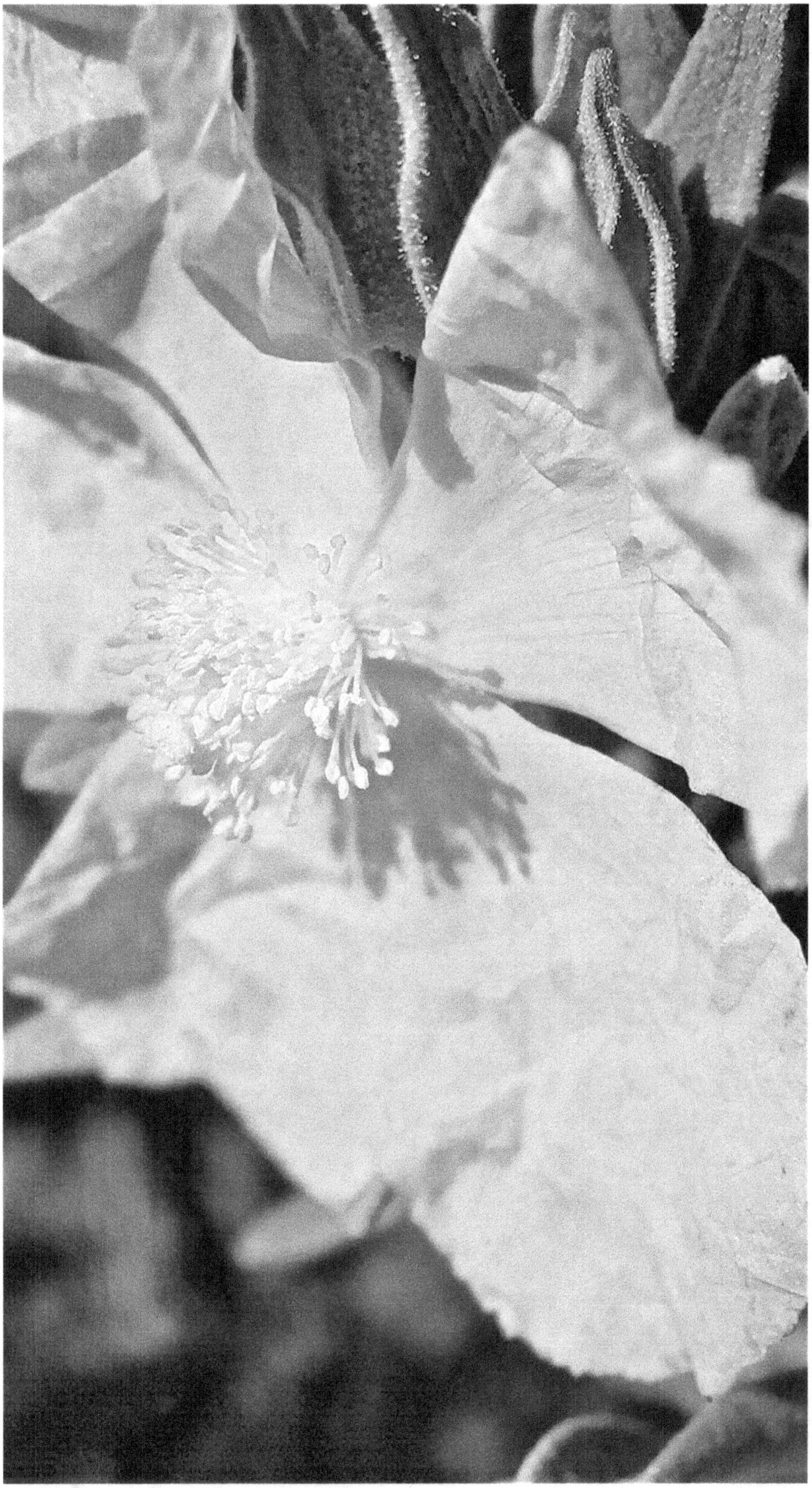

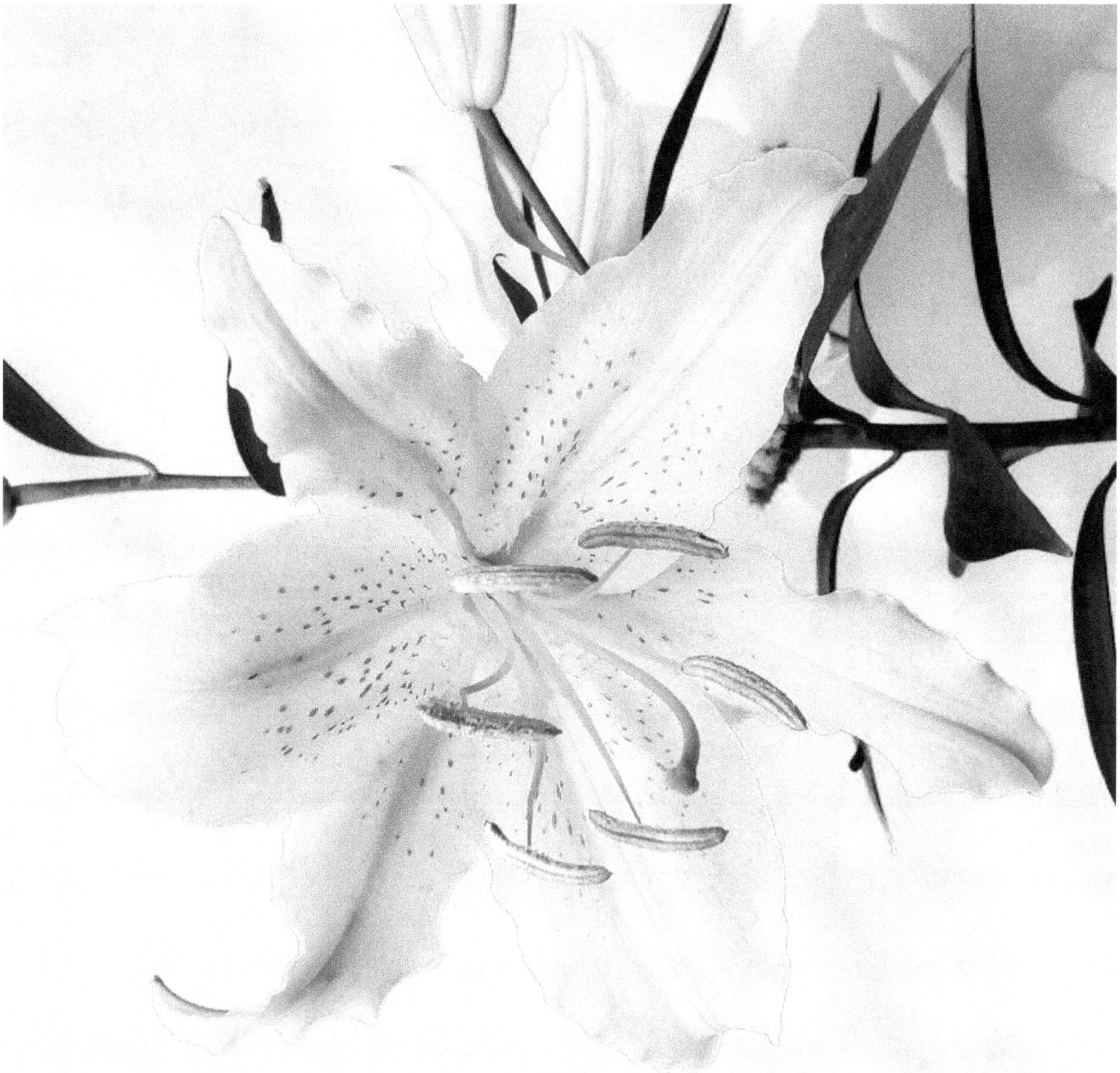

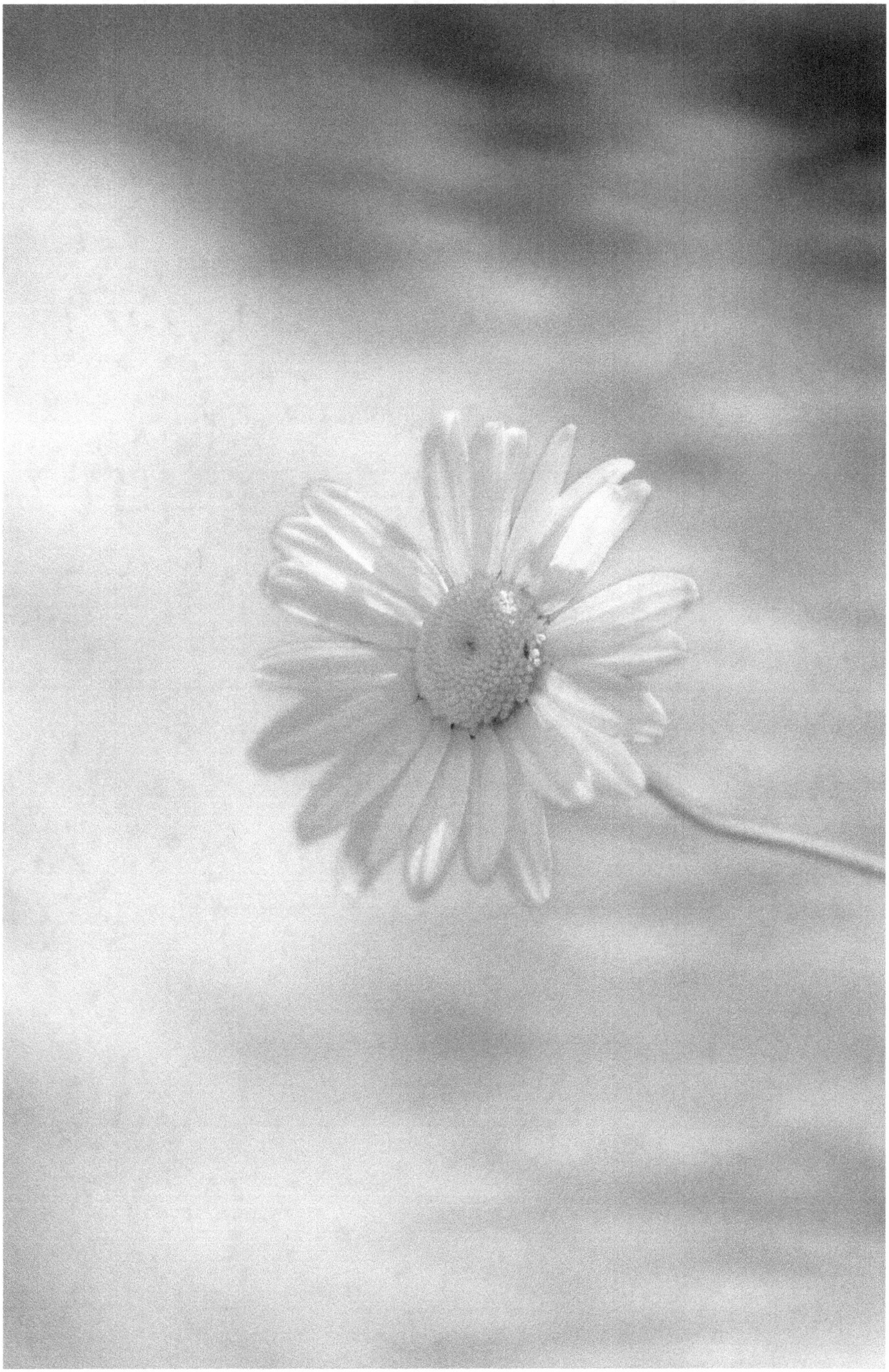

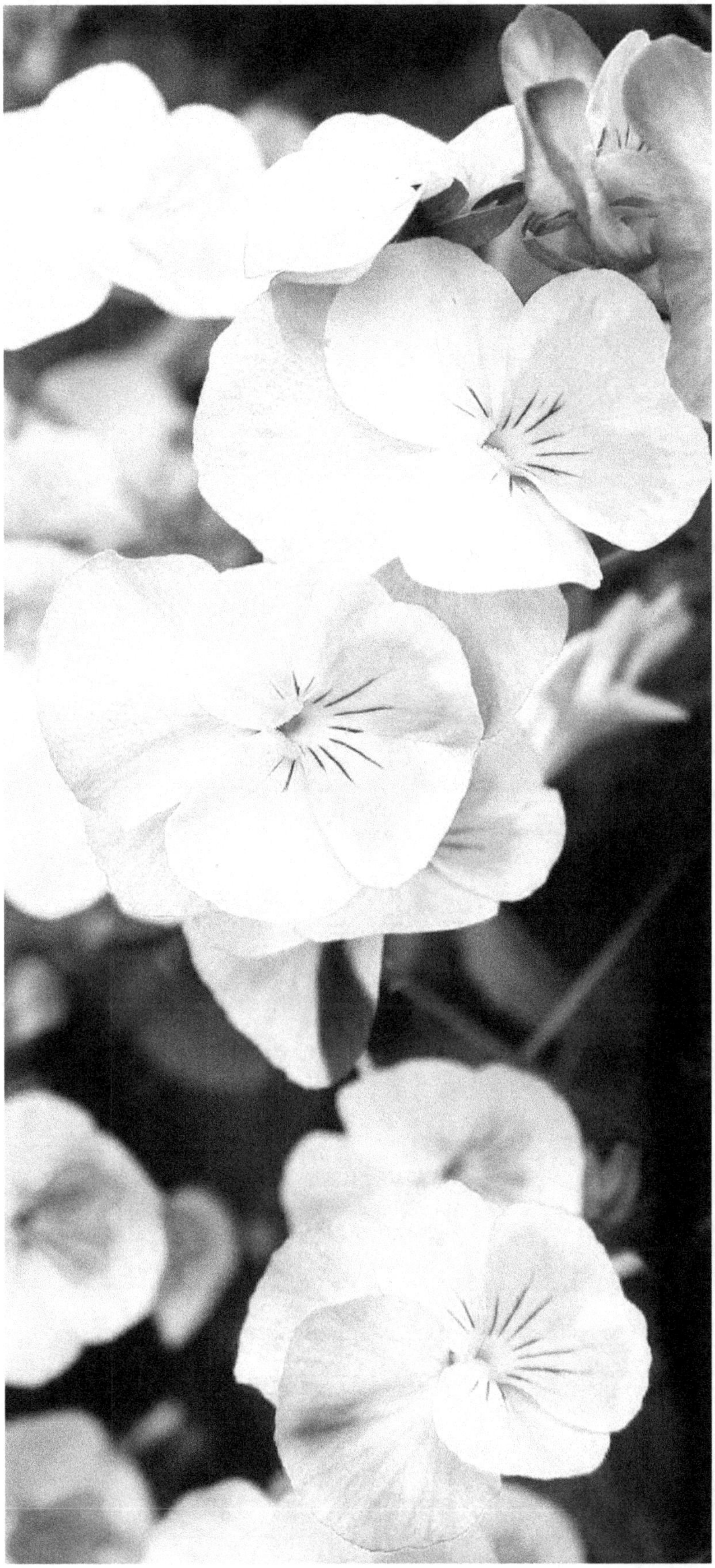

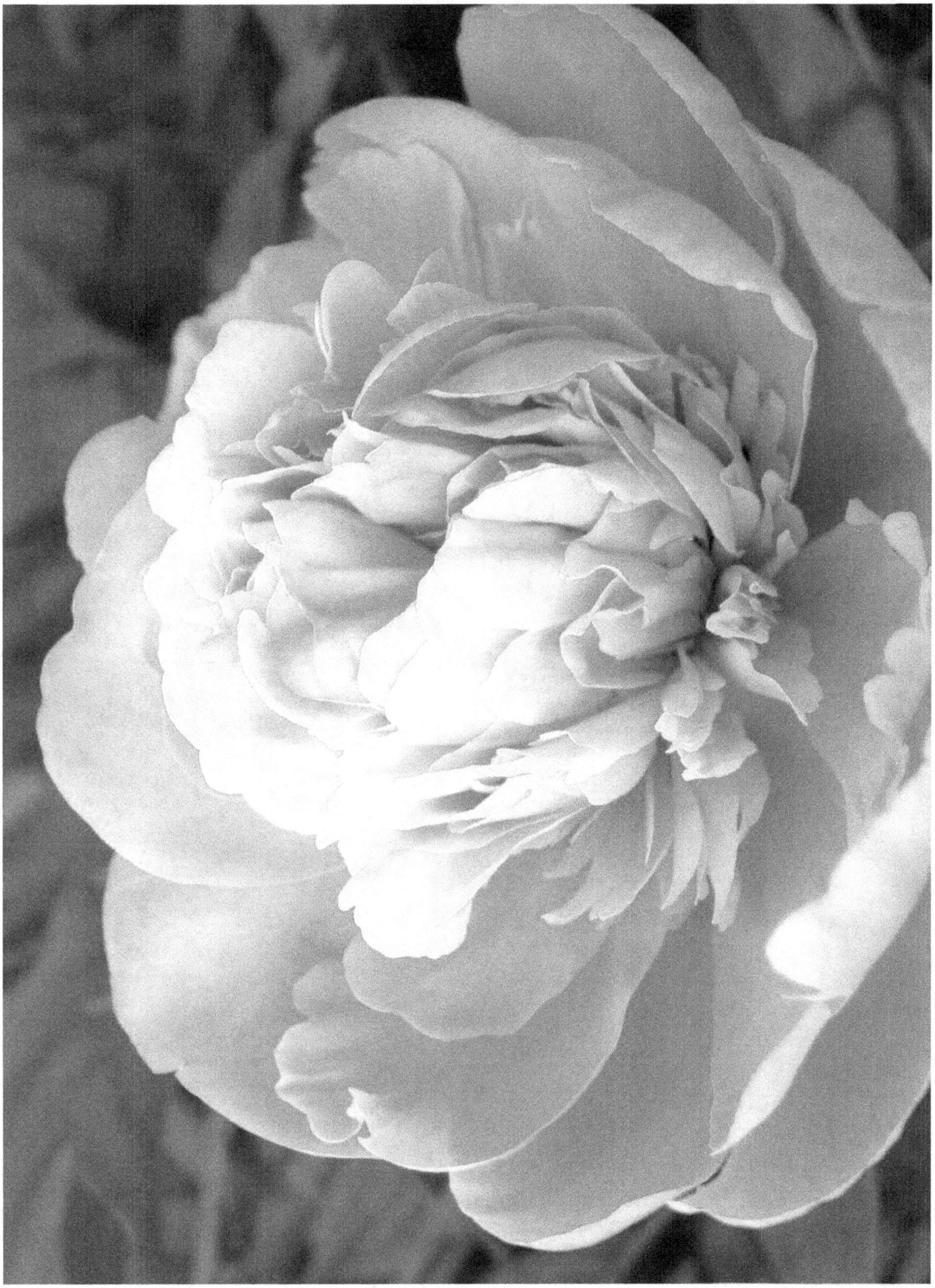

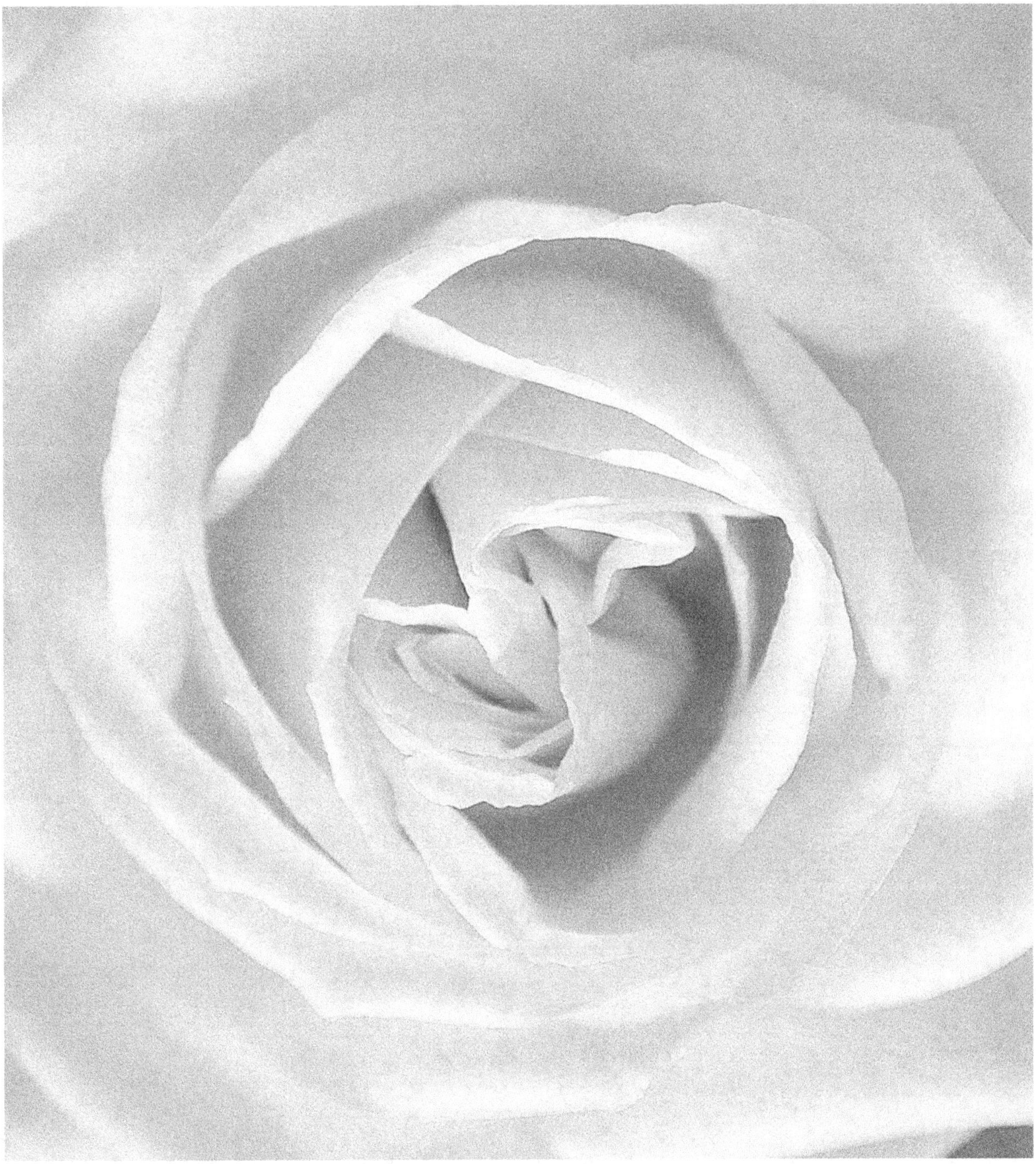

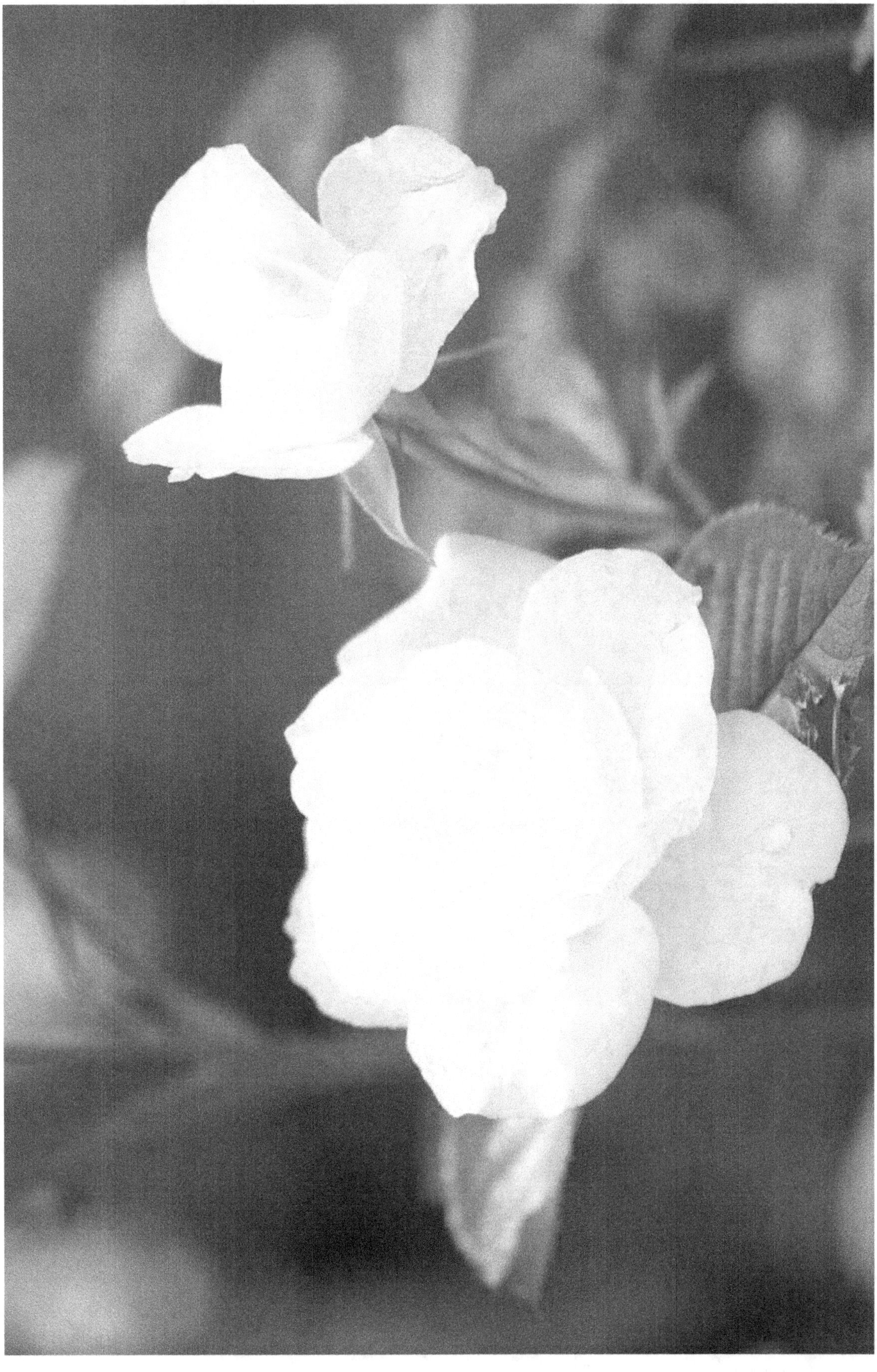

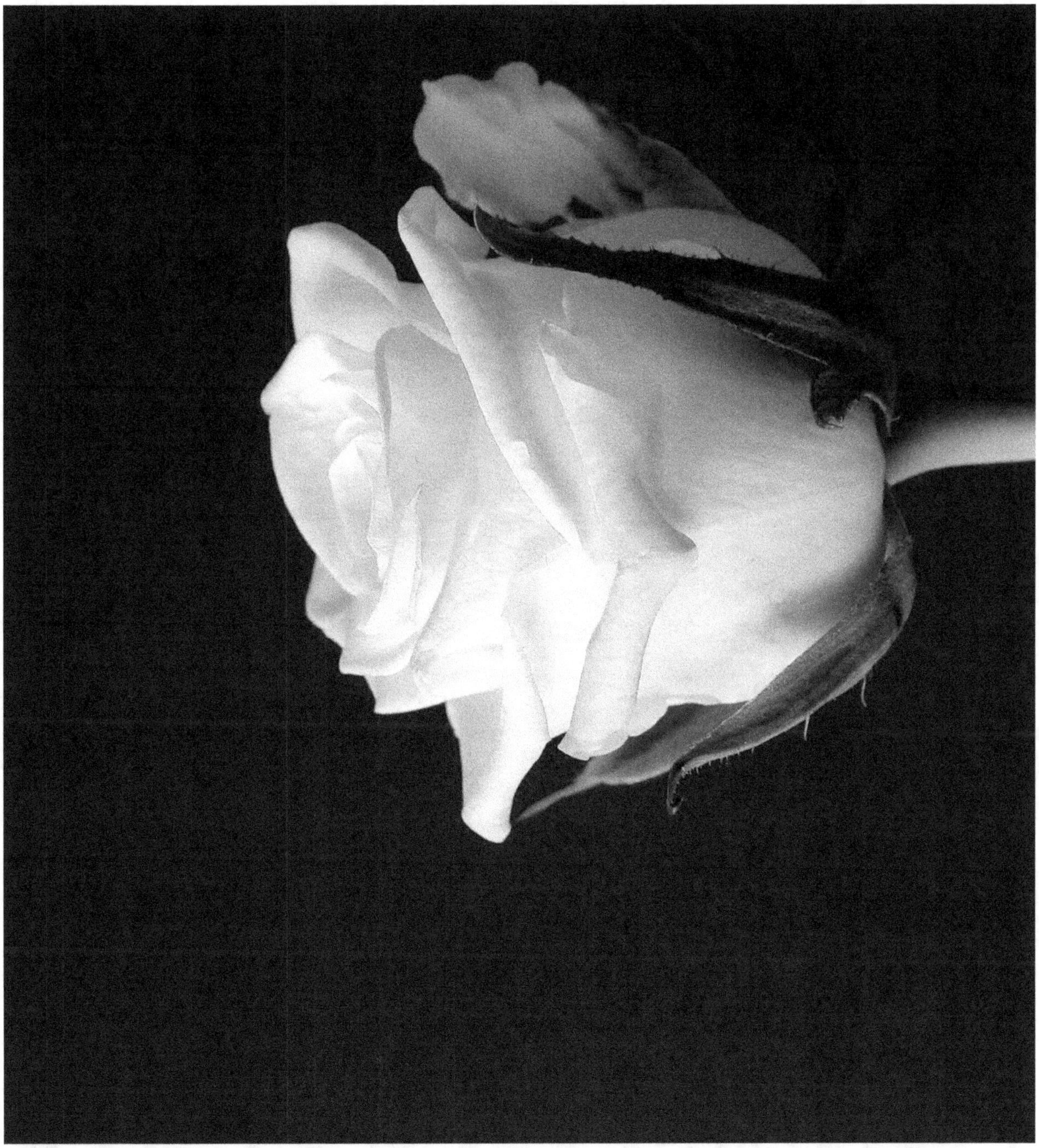

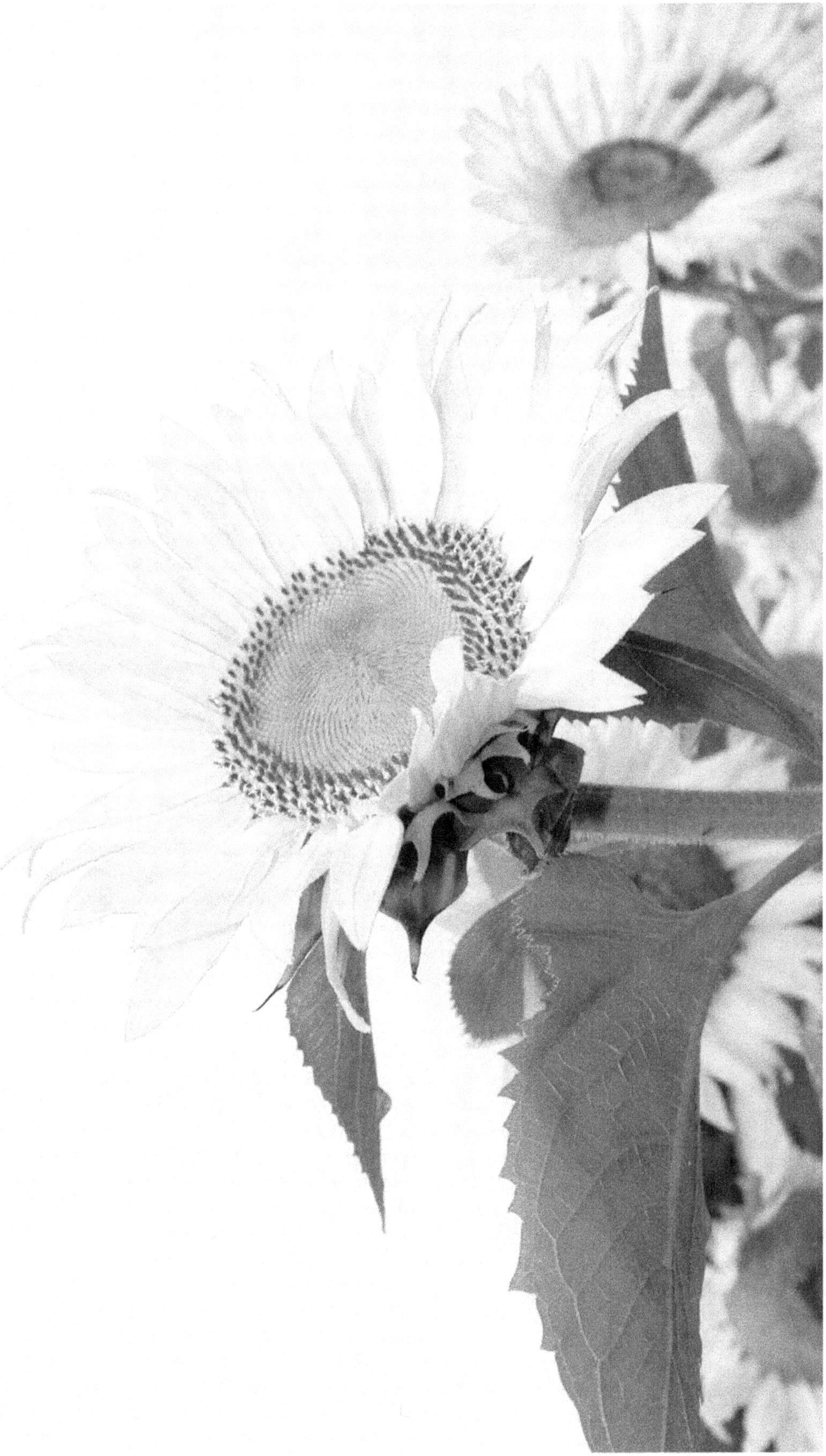

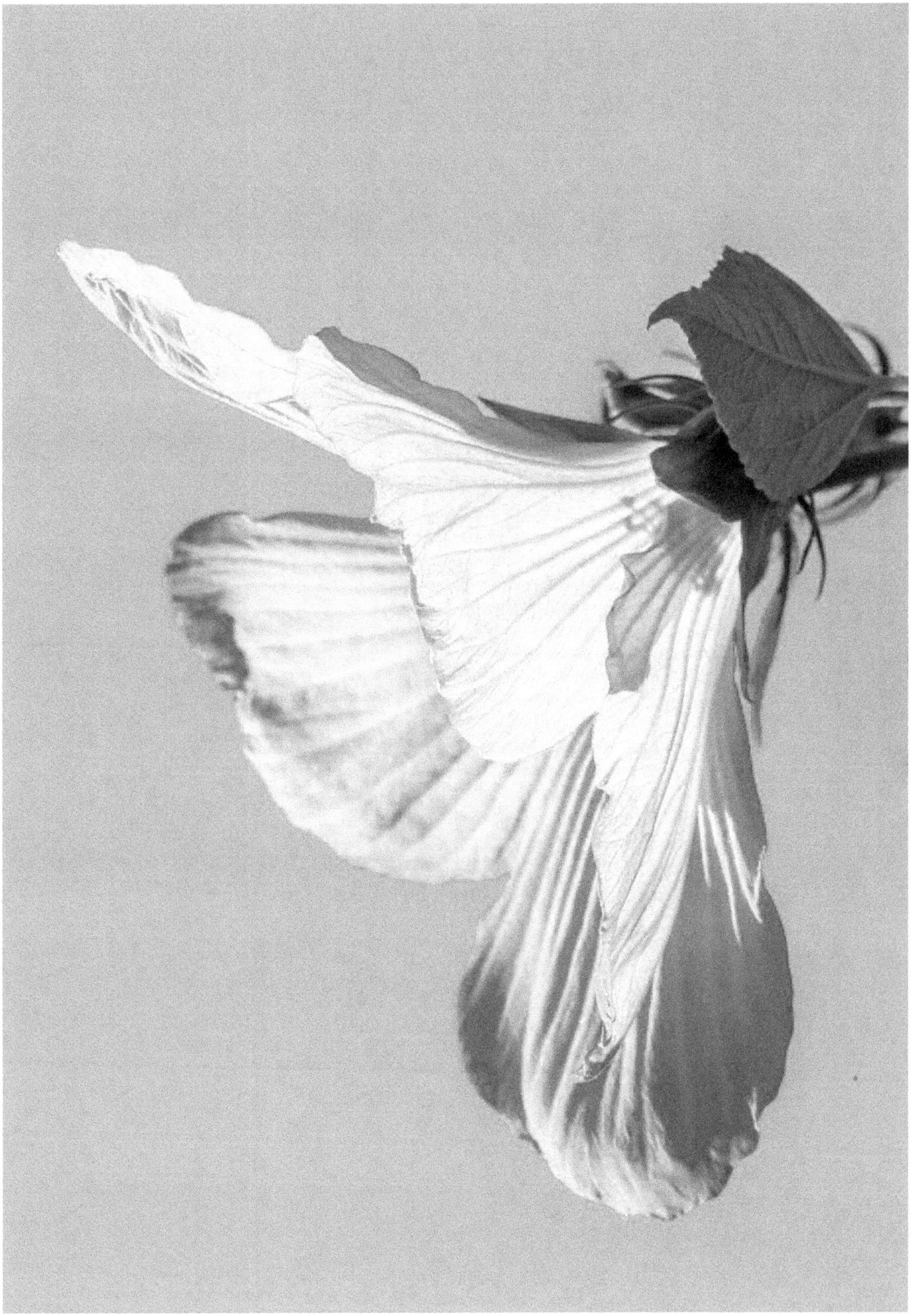

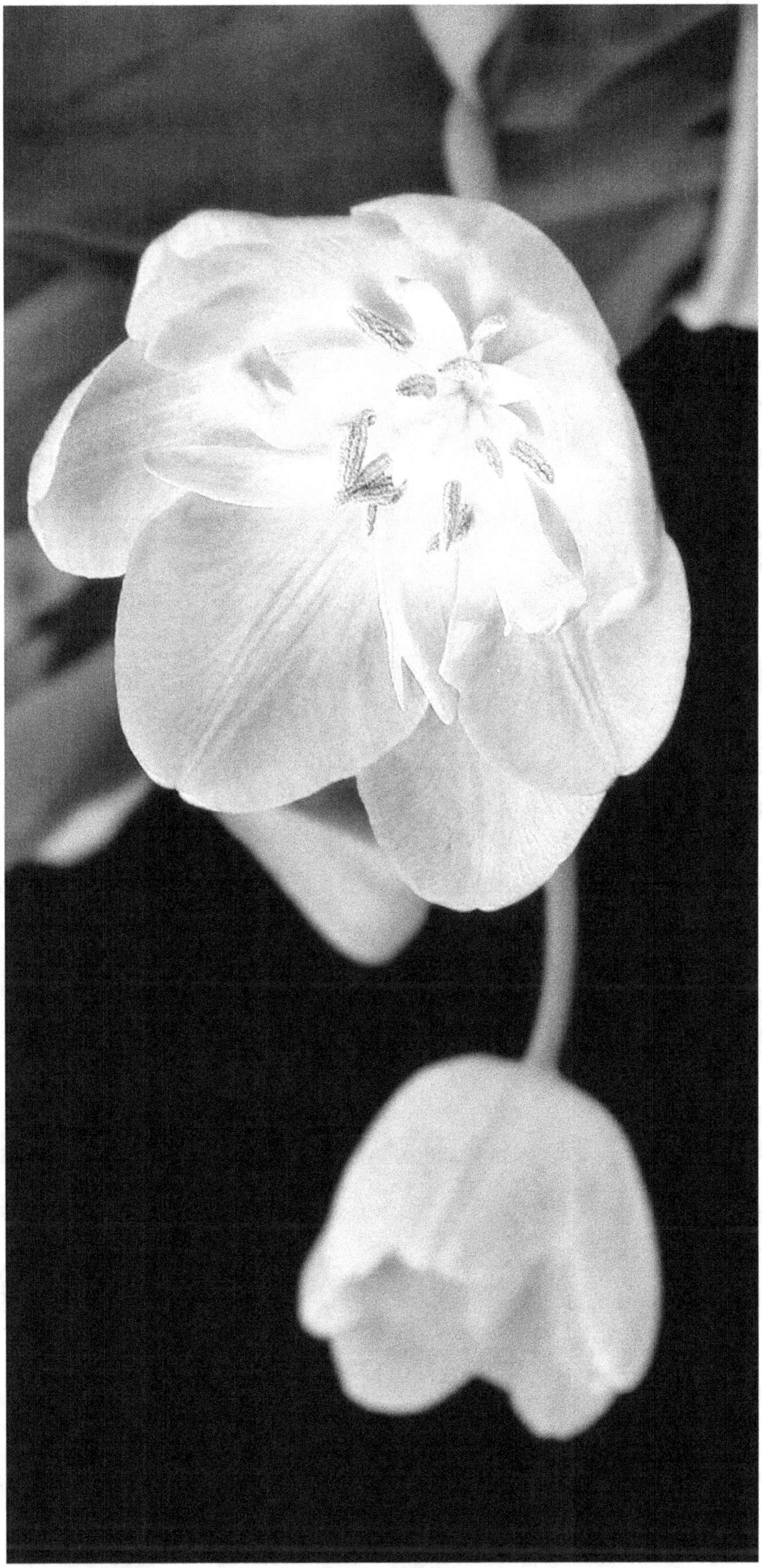

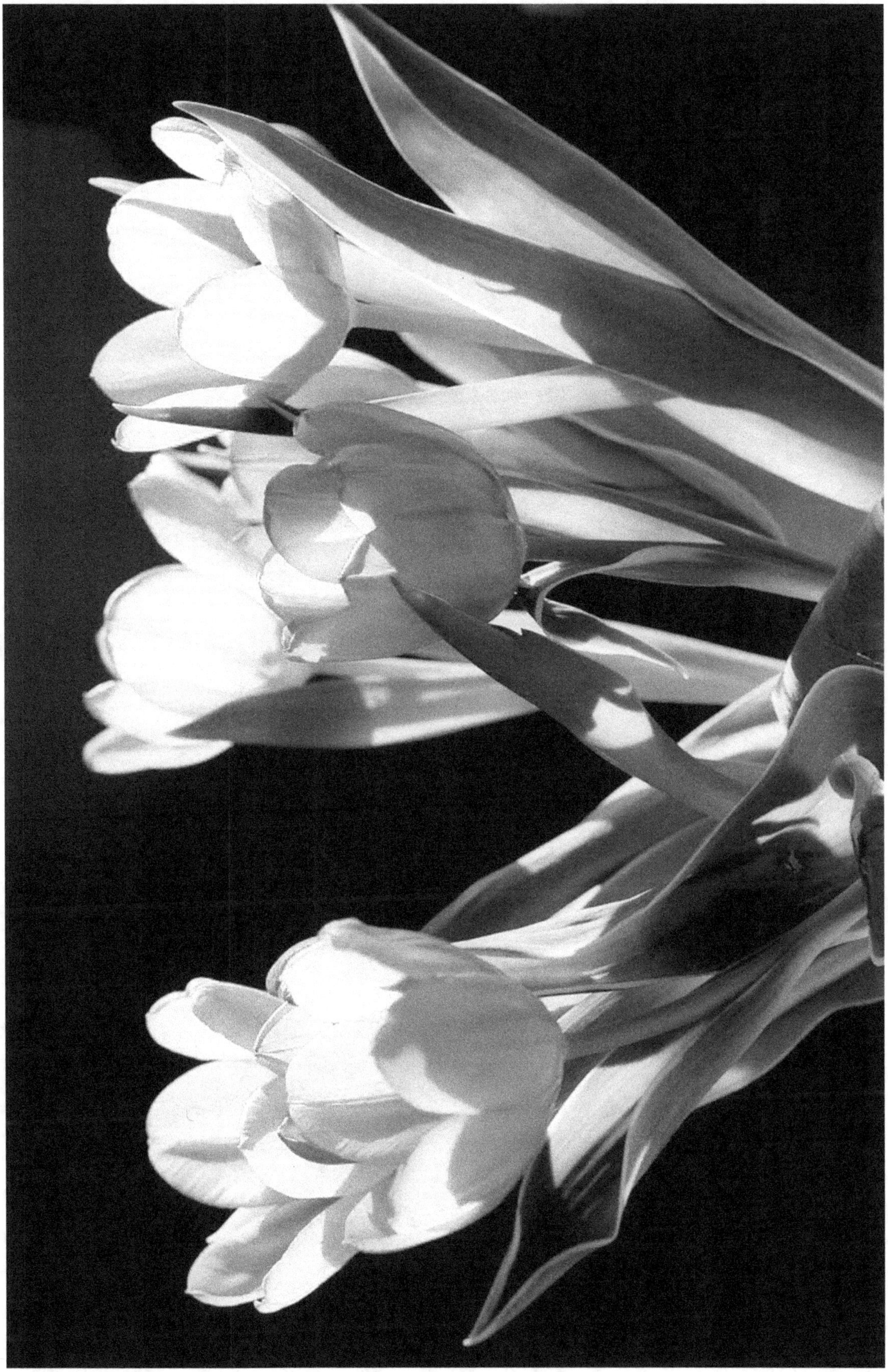

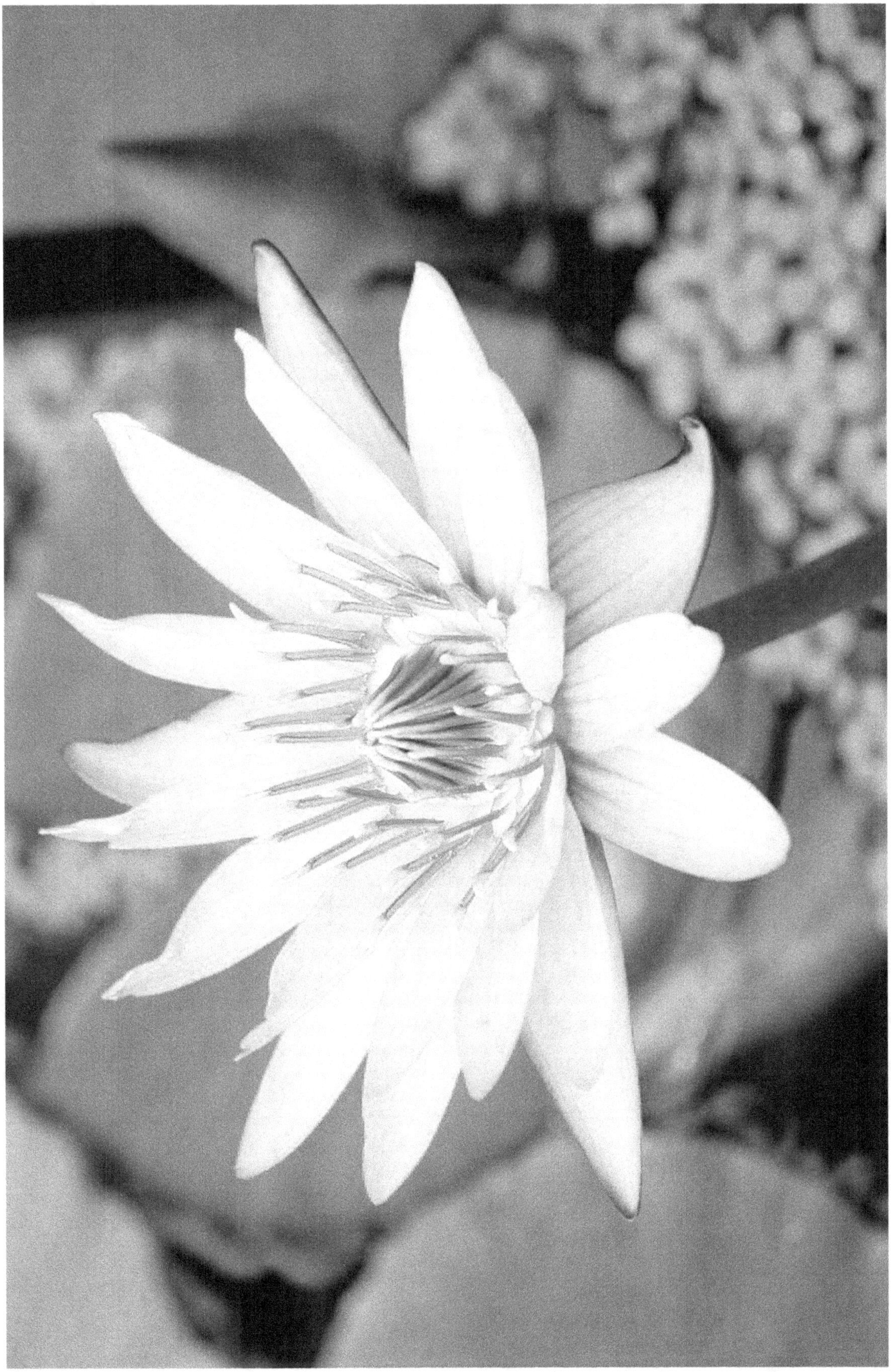

www.ingramcontent.com/pod-product-compliance
Lightning Source LLC
Chambersburg PA
CBHW081124280526
45787CB00007B/2976
* 9 7 8 1 5 3 5 0 6 8 7 3 4 *